Tending

ISBN:-13: 978-0615913421

Cover photography by Cynthia Piper.

Alrich Press
24600 Mountain Avenue, 35
Hemet, California 92544

Dedicated to Mark, love of my life.

Tending

Laura Grace Weldon

Aldrich Press

Contents

Putting By

Planting

Out of Body

Before I knew how to make my eyes march
in rows following shapes called words,
before I could cross the street
without a taller hand to hold,
I worked to stay in the small body
my being was given.

If not for careful attention I drifted.
Became the squirrel on a branch
muscles keen to leap
nose a nervous twitter, ever wary
though I sought
only furry playfulness.
Became J.P. down the street
licking lips already chapped and bleeding
jeering smaller children loudly
to silence a chest ribbed with sorrow.
This made it harder to hate
the bully he seemed.

At night I pulled blankets tight,
trapped my limbs under the covers
but still, the room grew
till my bed became a speck
and me, a traveler.
From a vantage point I didn't seek
I saw dark houses hunker on endless streets,
cars move past like glittering magnets,
within them people hauling heavy lives
when all around them
was this space any could soften into.

I pulled back and back and back,
searching for and sharpening
my own edges.
Even though I stay in this body
sometimes I drift
sliding through
as we all can
from me into you.

Rutabaga

You darken as my knife slices
blushing at what you become.
I save your thick leaves
and purple skin
to feed the cows.

A peasant guest at any meal
you agree to hide in fragrant stew
or gleam nakedly
in butter and chives.

Though your seeds are tiny
you grow with fierce will
grateful for poor soil and dry days,
heave up from the ground
under sheltering stalks
to sweeten with the frost.

Tonight we take you into our bodies
as if we do you a favor—
letting your molecules
become a higher being,
one that knows music and art.

But you share with us
what makes you a rutabaga.
Through you we eat sunlight,
taste the soil's clamoring mysteries,
gain your seed's perfect might.

Ruminating

Animals are incapable
of higher thought and emotion,
or so I was taught.

I don't suppose
Isabelle ruminates
as people do, observing,
mulling things over later.

I only know
she comes in for milking
yet flinches as the stanchion
clangs shut around her head.

Steps carefully
when chickens forage underfoot
but swings her head
to dispute a fallen apple.

Lets the barn cat sleep
atop her warm flank
and rises slowly, letting
him ride her broad back.
Softly lowing and nudging
Isabelle has taught,
warned, and comforted
each calf she has borne.

This year she nursed her son
till he outweighed her.
When he was taken away
she called all afternoon
at the gate he'd left.

Today as we approach
our noise splits the day.
Ducks rise from the pond,
a groundhog slips under the barn.
Isabelle, her hide a map
of unknown brown and white
continents, watches.

We rend logs apart
remarking on the wood's beauty
as we stack broken trees
into dark huddles.
We will unlock them
in fire and smoke,
we creatures who plan ahead.

Isabelle regards us
from the nearby fence line
her soft lips moving
as she chews, ruminating.

Our breath hangs in the cold air
smelling of her son
roasted with onions, herbs, and wine.

Why the Window Washer Reads Poetry

for Michael, who carried poems in his work shirt pocket

He lowers himself
on a seat they call a cradle, rocks
in harnesses strung long-armed
from the roof.

Swiping windows clean
he spends his day
outside looking in.

Mirrors refract light into his eyes
telescopes point down
photographs face away,
layers of dust
unifying everything.

Tethered and counterbalanced
these sky janitors hang,
names stitched on blue shirts
for birds to read.
Squeegees in hand they
arc lightly back and forth across
the building's eyes
descend a floor, dance again.

While the crew catches up
he pauses, takes a slim volume from his pocket
and balancing there,
36 stories above the street,
reads a poem or two
in which the reader is invariably placed
inside
looking out.

Santa Clara County v. Southern Pacific Railroad

Precedent for corporate personhood established by U.S. Supreme Court ruling, 1886.

What's alive seems puny
in darkness this large.
An engine's steaming eye wavers,
then train cars too big to fail
cartwheel down a wet hillside
in shrieking metal tantrums.
An embarrassment of merchandise
sprawls across quiet grass:
imported TVs, broccoli, children's shoes.

Before dawn, machines larger
than what lies
are ordered to a resurrection.
Silent crowds watch
cranes lift each hulking body
and bulldozers crush what's left
into unwatchable, uneatable, unwearable
mud-licked trash.

Lifetimes ago my uncle raced
behind trains with other poor boys
collecting fallen coal shards
for a few moments heat.
The day a car uncoupled,
spilling frozen sides of beef,
armed guards arrived to destroy the cargo
but hungry people pushed onto the tracks.
They bent gladly all the way home
bearing supper's heavy promise.

Torn hillside nearly empty, still
those who know what it is to be broken
stand on the crushed grass
staring at tracks
leading away from here.

Haying: June 12

I follow windrows as they curve
around the field's geometry.
Rows of cut red clover and timothy
lie yet unsquared.

Driving our ancient tractor, I'm satisfied
with a perfect turn, the roller coaster rush
of throttling up over ruts.
Our finances are precarious
as the glue holding together my glasses.
Still, the conjunction of deep blue and green
plus birdsong, equals peace.

My sons lift bales from the field
a smooth ballet of strength
that plays like baling twine
unrolling steadily through the day.
My daughter stacks teetering rectangles
as her father pulls the wagon,
head turned watchfully.
Afternoon light shines in their hair.
They call to one another, laughing as they work
voices held aloft as chaff's long glittering.

Even swallowing this day
I couldn't feel more whole.
Hay piles up in the barn's dark recesses
like stored sunlight.

Praying Kind

I'm not much for church-y praying.
Especially the kind where you say
somebody else's words,
expecting them to snag off you
like a match
dragged across the sandpaper
of your particular circumstances
so as to flare right up to heaven,
lighting your miseries
for some of God's attention.

But when a siren's whine cuts close
I can't keep myself from passing words through
my chest to add whatever holiness I possess,
saying "oh Lord give em strength,"
before turning back to shelling peas
or stacking firewood.

And I think it's like prayer
to farm, mindful
that plants and animals
need to be exactly what they are,
seeing as nature is God drawing circles
for us to learn the shape of things.

Still, when I pass a big dairy farm
where hundreds of cows never walk in sunshine,
never eat green grass
growing so close they can smell it,
never get to suckle their calves,
I put in mind the quiet peace

of our own cows on pasture,
and I send that peace out
to every confined creature.
If that's prayer,
then I'm the praying kind.

Stones, Letters, Ancestors

For my mother

A stone clangs against my hoe
as I pry it from soil and roots.
If we still talked every day I'd describe it to you,
how it's warmer than the air
with welcome heft, like a puppy or a baby,
and nearly round
though a jagged edge
opens to inner layers, gray streaked with blue.
Loss always reveals more.

But you're gone and clouds pass.
I still see creatures in them as you so often showed me.
Sidewalks ice over, then thaw without your concern.
I kneel in the garden, chop onions for dinner, drive
to the library, work and laugh and keep up with family
feeling the space you held,
as generations have always done.

My sister and I page through boxes of fragile letters
reading passages aloud. *This is my precious son Allister,*
who will be six years old this spring, God willing.
The resolute voice left to us in perfect cursive
holds time. We know her son stands still as she fastens
his collar, that he likes to scatter crumbs
for the birds, and when consumption takes him
she saves a lock of hair pressed in his favorite book.
Here, 100 years later, we shudder in sorrow.

My dreams are meals, leaving stories
that keep me fed these waking hours.
If I could, I'd describe this dream to you.
You are there, dark-haired and vibrant

at a festive table, seated with our ancestors.
Everyone is talking with merriment
unknown among the stones.
From here it looks like a celebration.

House Torn Asunder

A row of kitchen cabinets
tilts at the curb
one door open crookedly
to violet-patterned shelf paper,
a house inside out.

Women's hands curled
around those handles
as yours held mine
opening to peer into the depths
each ordinary day.

So necessary once, holding
what sustains
filled and emptied,
filled and emptied
taken for granted.

Naked wood reveals where
they were pulled away from walls.
Generously wide sides show
layers of peach and yellow paint,
like petticoats exposed to the street.
A hole torn,
a whole
rent asunder
dishes washed clean
of your fingerprints,
penciled notes on recipes
faded to smears.

May a pickup truck stop
and a man, arms strong as possibility,
lift these cabinets and drive them
toward the life
of some other kitchen
letting their hinges creak again
like song remembered.

Why We Walk the Dogs

Yawning, you say you're too tired
yet we can't refuse
brown-eyed pleading at the door.

Away from these walls
we more easily silence sorrow and trouble
by looking, only looking.

Cows in the lower pasture raise their heads as we pass.
An oriole alights on a hickory fencepost
twined with buttercups. The sun stretches
generous arms of light, cloud to cloud.

The old dog walks alongside
as the puppy bounds
ditch to hillside, joyously muddy,
collecting scents for his dreams.

When grief or fear catches in my throat
I remember to look at the sky
letting higher hopes
hover over our steps.

Then through evening brightness
dozens of blue green dragonflies
swoop around us
in some unknown ritual. We wonder
which of nature's perfect gestures:
migration, mating, defense
this may be.

Standing in the middle
of our complicated lives
we feel a lift of hope
requiring no effort
and turn toward home
wide awake.

Larger Stream

Seeking quiet, I picture a stream
where I try again and again to
empty the basket of my mind
into her current.
I'm here so often I hear the water,
breathe mist-tossed air.

Today our farm's creek is muddy with spring rain.
I stand on dirt smooth as hands across a worn apron,
a gesture made familiar by Lottie Borges
who lived next door when I was small.

She was old as women are no longer,
wore a house dress, support hose,
stiff laced shoes,
and carried
a longing left undone.

She wanted to climb in the seat of a big rig
just once, start it up and drive.
When she spoke the urge aloud
people laughed, though Lottie fiercely
imagined the engine's power
thrum through her body,
wheels turn onto the road.

She had nowhere to pour her desire
but in that passing stream,
a stream that breaks rock as it widens,
gains force until it becomes a river,
while she watched women
not much younger become

first on the stock exchange,
first to climb Mt. Everest,
first in the trades.

I think of that larger stream,
syllables pronounced easily now
though we don't know
who first spoke them.

I do know this water
flowing from our land
will join Little Sweetly Creek,
enter the Black River,
merge with Lake Erie,
then St. Lawrence River,
on its way to become the ocean.

Weeding

Tea Party Manners

Brittle ladies, faces a collage
of rouge, powder and lipsticked lines,
crushed me in perfume drenched hugs.
They had little to say to me except
You look just like your mother.

My grandmother's friends
drank from cups called bone china,
reached for cookies pale as their hair.
Jewelry hung large
on ridged fingers and raked necks.

Mindful of *speak when you're spoken to*
I swung my legs, lacy socks atop shiny shoes,
until my mother's reproachful eye stilled me.
Those long afternoons I measured
her pillowy form to my scrawny body
her dark French twist, my blonde braids
her sharp focus, my daydreams
her absolutes--good and bad, us and them
while I churned through questions wider than words.

Leaving those tea parties
I sniffed, leaning too close, until my mother said
Blow your nose like a lady.
It was her scent I sought, reassurance
that her face would not sag beyond recognition.
That she would never die.
On those days she smelled
like the soap we saved for guests
flower shaped, hard and dry in the dish.

I wasn't a good girl, a picky eater
lazy and ungrateful.
At night I was afraid not of the dark
but that there might never be light again.
In early pictures I incline toward my mother
like a plant far from the window.

Sniffing with allergies, I visit my mother today.
Angry with nursing home aides
she questions their character and breeding.
Her hands tremble on the bedclothes,
veins over bone over cotton.
She murmurs weather and weariness.
I lean in to hear underneath the words,
to find her.
My hair is up in a twist
my body has grown ever softer
and the past clatters in my head
like spoons stirring sugar in a china cup.

Trying To Be Good

Heavy on the counter
a chocolate cake weighed down
with buttercream frosting
darkened a glass dish.

She poured Maxwell House instant in her cup,
milk for us, and we sat at the Formica table
where I could see pictures
in the speckled surface:
camel, mountain range, upraised arm
holding a crooked staff.

> You're just like your father's side
> eat all you want
> never gain an ounce.

My tongue coated with oily sweetness
my belly didn't want
any more than swallowed bees,
I longed to drink my milk
pretending I was Heidi in the Alps
among goats and flowers,
to ride my bike Black Beauty,
card in the spokes his clopping hooves,
to be worthy of my mother's adoration.

> Finish your cake
> come on now
> before Daddy gets home.

So I ate the whole piece,
doing the container a favor.
Soon it would be washed clean,
not a dark smear anywhere
to show the load it carried.

Imaginary Boyfriends

Vital as lip gloss and the right jeans
our imaginary boyfriends were
always older and never anything
like boys in school—stupid, cruel or
never aware of us at all.

Oh you don't know him,
we'd explain.
Met him at my cousin's
over summer break.
He goes to another school.
Yeah, we're gonna take pictures
we keep forgetting.

Sometimes we'd roll our eyes
like Rachel had to be making
her guy up
but we gave her that right,
nodding as she told us how
they snuck out to meet
last weekend and what they did
in his backseat, deciding
our imaginary boyfriends
should have cars too.

These boys adored us.
Tender kisses,
long phone calls, gifts
bought with our babysitting money
and promises, beautiful promises.
Our boyfriends kept us
awake at night with

wanting so fierce
their faces became real.

After awhile we had to send them
away. They moved out of state
or joined the military.
We moved on.
Still, they wouldn't
get over us.
When boys didn't
call us back, didn't turn their heads
from the TV, didn't pay
child support, we knew
we were someone's first
and only love.

Our imaginary boyfriends
grow older with us.
Now they save lives,
direct movies, lead teams
to victory. Their eyes seek us out
from talk show interviews.
They whisper during sleepless nights,
of what might have been.
When we wake the next morning
to answer phones in an office
or stand in a checkout line
those imagined lives
rub against ours
awkwardly as two shy mouths
never kissing at all.

Chains, Bars

At four years old
I felt it in my throat.
The short chain slung around a tree
jerked as the puppy jumped,
each pull toward freedom
slamming eager barks to squeaks.
My voice cracked to a whisper.

At seven, I felt it in my legs
searching zoo paths
to find wolf eyes.
He paced head down, gaze unfocused
in a dark cement cell behind rusty bars,
his tight steps an indictment.
That day lengthened past my bones.

Now I feel it in my belly,
insides twisting at a glance.
You sit on the couch, clock staring
while your business fails.
You won't walk the farm
second mortgaged beyond us.

The children are quiet.
We look at you
not looking at us.
Your posture howls
of a man trapped
and we, your family,
keep our distance like jailers.

Making It Work

Everything is beige and brown,
color of cut apples left too long
in his house, yours too now, where we sit
you insisting *we're happy* while your hands
like frightened birds dart
to brush crumbs, crease napkins,
each flutter of your fingers reaching
farther across the table.

Framed parables, hers, yours too now
speak from walls crowded with flowered paper
and the air is weighted by old grief and Glade Plug-In.
I long to close my eyes halfway, see you through
veiled lashes or better yet, tell you this is a dream
you can wake from, a dream we can speak of
later, walking in the sunshine.

You get up to pour coffee and stand
still talking, still smiling,
leaving the counter between us.
Your hands curl a dishcloth
across that hard surface, absently
then fiercely, scrubbing one place
as if to bore all the way down
to dark forgiving earth.

Nest Unmade

We who
feathered out and left
long ago
meet on phone lines

squawking terms
so sharp they don't hold shape:
meds, PT, therapy

while you lie stranded
in a bed not your own,
hunched and aggrieved.

Even from an embrace
you draw back
as if from talons.

On a high tension wire
we shift and reshift
sister, brother, sister.

None of us speak
of the twigs, string and bright bits of memory
scattering in the wind,
we only remark on the wind itself.

If I could lift you for that flight
I would.

What She Saved

In a striped Vanity Fair box between crumpled tissue
lies a white satin honeymoon gown,
yellowed tags still attached.
Snapped shut in chic leather cases
wait unused compacts and pen sets,
wishes on cards tucked neatly inside.

Holding her necklace to my throat
the clasp gives way. Beads clatter apart.
I unfurl a silk fan to find intricate designs
fragile as moth wings
drifting slowly to the floor.

Everywhere I find what she saved.
Gifts too lavish, clothes too dressy, linens too formal.
I grieve anew as light falls
on each dusty object laid to wait.

Her choices fill this dark, closed-in house.
I touch each thing, lamenting,
until I see an equation.
Subtraction takes away,
revealing what hasn't been seen.
Her answer,
I am not this.

Tearing Down the Schoolhouse

Three days it took to demolish the front wall.
Sleek machines clawed at her masonry,
her heavy lintel,
leaving at first only scars
on a defiant body built to last.

Wooden staircases aloft nearly 80 years
left reaching no floor.
Walls where restless children stared,
knuckled open to the sky.
Driving by, I can't bear to look.

Her bricks are now ground to dust
not a swing left in the schoolyard.
Still each time I pass
I think of a struck bell,
how it resonates through ribs and spine,
as your voice rings in me.

Locust I

First--weighted air.
You pause,
awakened by the unknown.

Second--sound.
Winds rise into
hymns without words,
lives urged onward by jaws behind them.

Third--sight.
Slowly, then unrelentingly
the sky becomes a whirling torrent.
Sunlight shudders
and everywhere hungry locusts drop.

A curse, some cry
as shadows fall.
Mouths scour the land
leaving others to starve.

Manna, some cry,
nets ready and baskets
to harvest this delicacy.

Look into the darkness
there lies your salvation.

Locust II

Crackling like news
these recluses transform
from green-hued
to black and yellow,
shy to swarming,
plant eater to cannibal.

Seeking safety with others
exactly like themselves
they hurtle onward
more away than toward,
building in mass
wreaking the havoc
fear always does.

Bosnia, Rwanda, Darfur.
Hate radio, Guantanamo,
the end of Posse Comitatus.
The simple food of John the Baptist
driven to swarm.

Breathing the Deepwater Horizon

I wake smothering.

Dark outlines of my grandparents'
carved bed and your sleeping body
calm me, though my breath is still caught
with those in the ocean's clogged room.

Tipping my head, mouth open
like any organism seeking air,
I think of plankton and krill
swirling on poisonous currents.
Of resolute creatures steering
by ancestral maps to gulf water,
eyes keeping watch
long after their hearts stop.

Breath scarce, body
a shrieking whistle,
I hear waves preach:
do unto the whole world
as you would have
the whole world do unto you.

Bless you bless you bless you
I murmur, tipping forward
to rock as the crazy do
and those mad for God
and those who lull tiny babies.
I breathe in oily darkness,
try to exhale light.

Ways of Speaking

I'm weary of those who talk
in slogans stamped and packed
by someone else, like
long distance truckers paid to drive
without knowing the weight
hauled onto that dark highway.

I want to walk, instead
where I can read the body's slow knowing.
Where each thing watched long speaks aloud.

A spider tossed by the breeze casts
one strand thin as faith. As it takes hold
she dances between twigs and waits
within a design both beginning and end.
When the web breaks she starts again
tiny legs speaking in ways
we're meant to hear.

Harvesting

Design Revealed

Heart leaping faster
than my limbs
I answered each cry,
rocking tiny ones
till lashes closed
into worlds past me.

I nodded at mantras chanted
by women my mother's age
enjoy them while they're young
this time goes too fast
though so weary
my skeleton ached for rest.

Motherhood's origami
folded and creased me
in unfathomable patterns,
as together we composed songs
for the Milky Way
on late night walks,
blessed insects we set free
from window-bound prisons,
danced through days
far from time's imagination.

Mantras come true.
Those little ones now
lean over me,
pausing gently
before hurrying
toward worlds beyond.

Last night
I dreamed of fallen fruit
ripe unto bursting.
I offered this bounty to children
but in house after house
they had been fed.
Waking,
I see design revealed.
I feel the beauty
of greater unfolding.

Perspective of Distance

For a son grown and gone.

So short a time
does light speak
this way.

Earth's whirl
past the sun's
blessed fire
lends meaning to stone.

Here on this planet we heave and strain,
wresting nature into shapes we choose:
straight lines, perfect squares, calendars, plans.

When aching from your absence I walk
scuffling pebbles along one such road
thinking of how you look into everything
fiercely as sunlight shines through rock
hewn by ancient ones
in Uxmal, Newgrange, Chaco Canyon.

One whole week in September,
a gift of latitude and earth's tilting axis,
the sun sets exactly
at the street's end.

Like a shimmering band of ribbon
it lies across these shapes:
pastures, barns and fences,
illuminating in gold
the road you can take home.

How to Pick Blackberries

for Jean

Wait, till wanting the dark taste
waters in your mouth
then walk through the day's heat with
hymns of insect people all around, walk
where your steps silence rustling creatures.
Don't be careful. Lean into brambles,
prickers tugging at your jeans, snagging your shirt.
Reach far to accept these wild offerings.

Hear her voice saying
"You want em good and ready
so they fall in your hand, dead ripe"
though you can't remember
ever picking berries together.
Her spirit is a reminding one
and she's right, you think,
dark fruits hang heavy among their red-bodied sisters
releasing at your touch
like the saved drop into baptismal waters.

Blackberries stain your fingers
passing to basket, passing to lips.
The tender squish and grit of seeded fruit
still alive, brings tears to your eyes
or maybe it's that dog a ways off
barking his wants.
You think of her, mouth pursed
like a bread bag pulled tight.
You know life cost her dearly
but remember best her eyes,
always looking ahead.
She would have liked to pick blackberries today.

Step farther in where shadows are cool
where blackberries hang heavy
just past briars. Thorns scratch your face
and tear your clothes, but don't give up
you can pick more here.
Blood marks your forehead,
mosquito songs rise
over the beat of cicadas and crickets.
If you trip, hold the basket
to your chest,
hold it gently while you tumble.

Then go on, gather blackberries
one by one, take all you need
while listening to her voice in your head,
"Dead ripe, oh Lordy yes,
dead ripe" and hope it was that way
when her time came,
so full and sweet
that she was ready to fall.

A Pilgrimage

for Angela Cory

The rituals are unfamiliar.
Sharp odors, bursts of sound,
waiting, more waiting.
I want to flee.
Yet when called
I sit at a mirrored face
shrouded in black.

In the ICU
I leaned close
to your faint breathsounds,
your slack mouth,
your eyes watery and unseeing,
leaving words of thanks
outside your ears.

You always
wore heavy perfume
heavier earrings
and a perfect manicure. You
favored rhinestone studded sweaters
but left unjudged
my long hair, bitten nails, frayed jeans.
You stood behind women
all day, complimenting,
smiling, styling hair.

Now the comb tugs, blade cuts.
Strands slide down this black cape.
I watch a broom join

gray, blonde and black wisps
in a moving collage
as women's voices
speak to reflections.

I enter your world
to honor it
sacrificing
a hair's length
while you hold your breath
seeking greater beauty.

Doorways

For the living memories of those lost in China's Sichuan earthquake, 2008

Here, crickets and frogs call
in the spring breeze
like notes stirred from the pipa.

I can only hold your pictures Mingmei.
You, bright baby faced in the snow.
Then a laughing boy by the water,
so soon, a man squinting in the summer sun.
Your eyes look through time.

A red bird alights
on a crab apple branch
singing in the warm sunshine.

When I sleep I see you, Mingmei
standing in my doorway,
holding your son,
although he lives
and you are beyond.

The fragrance of honey locust
hangs in the air
luring butterflies and bees.

There are many doors, Mingmei
many thresholds to cross.
Here, we approach
through dreams, offerings, prayer.
We see that passage
true as a field of tall grasses
waving in the wind.

New To The City

Hammer, anvil, and stirrup
tremble in your ears.
Horns and back up beepers
cut through layers of clothing,
past skin, piercing you again and again.

Pavement caps a prisoned forest
where soil bears the city's heft
and seeds lie waiting
for a lost sun to resurrect them.

You want to look at the crowd
as you might a painting,
slowly, seeing each face.

Maybe sound doesn't disappear
but drifts outward in ever widening waves.
As you walk along ringing streets
you sew notes into the folds of this city's
loud curtain, imagine them fluttering
through unknown expanses
like Earth's gift to a quiet universe.
Even if they fall far short
why not whistle?

So Soon

I'm reminded of an egg's
brief perfection.
What grows within
must crack what contains it.

At seventeen
you squint at farther horizons
bits of childhood still
in your hair, your walk, your laugh.

Behind you
this place we fashioned,
each twig bent to nestle you
just so, will ever after be
changed by your flight.

Haying: June 10

When I committed a childish impoliteness
I was asked,
Where were you raised, a barn?
Any answer increased my infraction
but Jesus lay in a manger
and He was holy.

When I fibbed
I was told liars were *filthy dirty,*
if I wasted my savings
I heard the perils
of becoming *dirt poor.*
I scrubbed when entering
because *people like us*
don't go unwashed
even though dirt
grew the roses my mother loved,
dirt held the bodies of those who left us.

When grown,
I dressed my own little ones in overalls,
clean ones mind you
but my mother disapproved
they look like farmers,
not like smart children.

There it was, root of the tree,
generations soiled
with hardship
deemed ignorant.

I came to the old ways
with time
and preaching of stones,
though both speak slowly.
Some make journeys
to Mecca, Bodh Gaya or Jerusalem.
Others trace all the way back
to blessed dirt.

I drive our tractor, a 1948 Ferguson,
under vivid skies.
Trees lining the field offer shade
like a benediction
each time I turn.
Behind me the tetter
tosses drying hay.
Redwing blackbirds dart around us,
a young deer near the woods
regards us, serene faced.
Underneath 17 acres of cut hay
grasses continue growing,
unchanged by the temporary labyrinth
we mark in rows as we drive
around and around,
circling ever inward.

Life Transferred

'Dig deep,' he tells them.
Even bent over shovels
the boys tower above their grandfather.
Light shining on their bodies
shadow his frail form.

He casts each perennial out
to ease his labors, he says,
although these blooms seem
unbidden reminders
in purple, blue, pink.

Unsure the young heed advice
he repeats, 'Preparing the ground
is everything,' then sends us off
plants trembling the journey
bare in boxes on the backseat,
far from soil's embrace

Once home the boys haul manure
in a battered blue wheelbarrow
past beehives and barn,
through scattering chickens.
With dark loamy offerings
they tuck in each plant as prescribed.

Around the house green shoots now emerge
pastel-hued buds unfurling in shy grace.
Inside, children sprawl in sleep.
Faces like theirs smile bravely
from sepia pictures

I lift out of newspaper nests.
Everywhere evidence
that life transferred
blooms.

Sacrifice

for Chris Niedzwiecki

You don't believe me
but there will come a time:
you will want
to kill him
she said to her only daughter
over the newborn's bald head.

The woman's weary blue eyes
didn't round off the truth,
any more than old tales
brought from Poland. These
weren't stories of princesses
and magic leading to love,
but stories of long winters
and hard work
leading to wisdom.

When you do, she said,
call me.
I'll come
no matter what.

The daughter repeated her
mother's words
to friends and family,
stabbed anew
with each retelling.
What a thing to say
about my first baby,
her first grandchild.
I am not my mother.

She sharpened
her resolve with soft baby kisses

warding off the prediction
through weeks of diapers and
nursing, through
wide-mouthed squalling
and arched baby smiles.
But after another long night
of inconsolable crying
she unloaded that baby
harshly in his crib,
told her husband
I don't want
to be a mother any more.

Brushing his teeth,
he said, if you feel that way
maybe we should put him
up for adoption.
To her angry face in the mirror
he added, Call your mother.
Or I will.

Early, before the sun was up
this woman put a coat over her nightgown
and ran across snowy backyards
of her Cleveland neighborhood.
Sleep, she told her daughter,
staying all day,
child in her arms.

That grandson,
his eyes her shade of blue
stands tall and gracious
at her funeral.
He's leaving
for Harvard Divinity School
where he will surely learn
stories of sacrifice
and love and anger
that hold a people together
though he
knows them already
in the steady pulse
carrying her blood forward.

Perfectly Good

The chair broke years ago
leaving jagged oak
at its topmost edge.
Repairs never held and
here my youngest son sits
his face lit from within.
If I could, I'd fashion everything broken
into a greater whole, forming
a bridge to his highest possibilities.
Instead he eats supper
with sharp wood bristling at his ear
and when I suffer it aloud
the boy says, "It's perfectly good."

This was the mantra of my childhood.
Spoken over fat and gristle
left on the plate till I forked those last bites
in my reluctant mouth. Invoked with each
hand-me-down, even though Jennifer's
mother made me wear suspenders
at her house to spare her my sagging trousers.
Implied in a fistful of stubby No. 2 pencils
my schoolteacher father saved
from the classroom trash can,
the same ones my mother darkened
her eyebrows with each morning.

Today my son helped with yard work
at my childhood home, then stopped
CSI-faced, to hold up a dark loamy figure.
My mother dismissed it casually,
"Oh, the overcoat
in the azaleas."

Her father's moth-eaten wool coat,
good tailoring still apparent in the shoulders,
had been too good to discard.
Instead it was perfectly suited
to smother weeds
forty long years.

Standing next to her in that doorway
I knew identity as something
broader than a name.
This is who we are.
Resilient enough
to chew the fat, hitch up our pants,
and raise our brows--- smoothing the way
for our children the best we can.
I grew up missing my grandfather,
yet all the while
his coat lay
right outside the window
arms spread wide,
keeping a place for flowers to grow.

Putting By

Hard Frost

It's there, right past the impulse to give up.

It turns apples, small, pocked with holes
into pie and cobbler
breathing spice through the kitchen.

Gathers butternut squash, turnips, and beets.
Using the worst first,
putting the best by.

Picks frost-bitten broccoli plants
as edible bouquets for cows.
(They pluck dark leaves with soft lips
and crunch on the stems in quiet satisfaction.)

Salvages the green tomatoes to make fiery curries.
Uses the last bit of honeycomb, the shriveled peppers,
the whey left after cheesemaking.

It lies within
the poor harvest, the wilt,
the bad spots, the lean times.

I won't give up
on you either.

Wedding Urn

You'll get a silver ice bucket with tongs,
pricey-looking but so poorly made
the one time you use it
some hidden seal will leak
leaving water all over the nice
mahogany table your grandmother left you
the one you didn't want
but don't want to mar either.

Eleven unreturnable gifts,
etched frames and embossed albums
you'll tuck in the backs of cupboards
and bottoms of drawers, where
they will take up more and more space,
kept only because the date
of your couplehood
is too potent a talisman to
leave in the trashbin or charity shelf.

Kitchen appliances, lots of them,
most with digital screens reminding
time blinks with a blank face.
And linens in colors
matching your first apartment long
after you've moved away.

What you won't get is a beautiful vessel
its use unknown to you at first.
You'll need such a container.
Dreams split into fragments.
Plans flare, then burn to soot.

Gather the grit with your fingers
away from eyes,
away from the marriage bed,
to seal in an urn
stronger than promises.

Driving Through Fog

Fallen clouds hover
like ghosts on the street, willing
my headlights to glare back at me.
Sometimes illumination
obscures the way.

Growing up I knew where my father was.
He whistled, he sang,
he talked to plants while gardening
and cars while tinkering.
One night, driving
through fog he called pea soup
he explained how lighthouses
help ships navigate.
Their lights don't shine
in one place, they sweep
across all possible paths.
They speak in foghorn voices
I'm here,
I'm here,
I'm here.

He piloted the car past signs,
buoys above a lost road.
Blasted the horn before each bend,
waking the night
in a delicious game of make-believe.
I don't remember where we were going
only our steady ship,
only his hands on the wheel.

Object Lesson

18 and in love
I heard
Too young.
Won't last.

Yet each solid thing unwrapped
from fussy wedding paper
made it real.

The cutting board
too thin
split into kindling.
Paint chipped off leaky flowerpots
we used till they cracked.

Bath towels, coarse and cheap,
wore down to barn rags.
Bed sheets, gone to tatters, were torn
to tie tomato plants and peonies.

One last gift, a satin-edged coverlet
we saved for good till every other blanket
fell to pieces. Pretty but polyester,
it too frayed to shreds.
Nothing temporal
remains inviolate.

All that's left are
clear glass canisters
holding exactly what we put in them
right here on the counter
for us to see
each day of our long marriage.

Aluminum Epiphany

Spreading his fingers
over roofing samples,
hands soundless
against metal slick
as his promotional pitch
the salesman says,
Aluminum is the mineral
Mother Nature and Father Time
use to make gems.

His voice moves on to
warranties and prices,
though his words
send
me
journeying.

I see
archeologists of the future
find long-buried suburbs
shining with inexplicable
treasure.
They uncover houses
sided in emeralds,
beer cans transformed
into opal cylinders,
lawn chairs of topaz,
ruby cooking pots.

They brush away
the perilous dust of that age,
careful to decontaminate

before returning home
to their children
who dream of ancient people,
awe-struck
at what it must have been like
to grow up
in the heart of
such indifferent opulence.

Dreams of Mice

Brains of sleeping mice reveal
to science, unwittingly,
that scent locks in memory
like Proust's tea and cake.

While lab coats scan, measure
and tabulate in chambers
scrubbed of odor,
tender-limbed mice dream
and reminisce.

Today's autumn air conjures
toast my mother made,
starlings swooping in unison,
and you, the comfort of your smell
in the bed where
our bodies mingle.

If baby mice curl in our closet
among boxes and blankets, surely
our scent enters their dreams,
lingering through their small
remembering lives.

Awake As You Sleep

Lying together, having made
something warm and forgiving
out of our years,
I pull close
against the cold ahead.

It doesn't matter, you say,
we're together now.
And after, well,
you believe whatever
you want. Me, I'll lie
in the dirt.
It is enough to have this, now.

And you sleep.

I don't want much.
Grateful for red knuckles from dishes,
splinters from firewood
the pinch from paying bills.
This life lets me tend my babies
and kneel in the garden.
But I am greedy to resurrect us
from that ground.

I say
we are more
than flesh can hold.

But you don't wake.

I imagine us ascend
to that promised bliss.

Or onward
where I search for you in every gaze
to grow, struggle, soften,
all over again.

Then I envision your dreamless eternity,
each molecule
separating. Forgetting,
forgetting as
mineral, water, air
turn our essence into light.

Small Bed

When you turn off the light
the room melts,
butter in night's hot pan.
We talk as the familiar sneaks back
wearing shy outlines.
You say,
because our bed is small,
we carry night's
long touch through the day.

It's true.
Your skin is my address.
Your inhale my exhale.
Surely there are times
our eyelids flutter
as we lie here two bodies
dreaming one dream.

Forgetting Names

I can't call up the familiar name
of our vet, who walked out back
with us through heavy snow
to check our feverish cow
in this day's quickening darkness.
My skittering memory
only shows me
his thick hair and kind gaze,
his hand gently resting
on our old dog's head,
a blessing easily bestowed.

No name comes to my lips
although somewhere
a space in my mind
prompts the letter D.
Eyes closed,
I drift into that space
untangled
like a fish free of a net
swims gratefully into open waters.

There I remain, no thought at all
for long moments, when somewhere
behind my eyelids I see
a complicated garment
sagging at the shoulders
where it's held
as if by invisible hands.
I know this
is the lifetime my soul wears.

Vastness like a perfect secret
stays with me
as I open my eyes,
remembering of course
we're outfitted in ordinary guises,
going by names
as if simply human.
And I recall the name he wears.
It's Dave.

Doorknobs

In memory of D.H.

Rain shreds his words,
syllables dissolving
past language.
Grass surrenders to mud,
threatening to toss the living
on the ground's slick tongue
toward your grave's throat.

When your faith in healing died
you gambled on promises of eternity
casting fearful dice
in all directions
heaven... samsara...nirvana
hoping to believe,
drawing only this man of the cloth
who now stands a stranger in front of us.

Nights later, waking in a dream
I see doorknobs everywhere.
Their differences are perfection.
Smooth wood darkened
by the polish of many hands,
crystal faceted like jewels,
white porcelain mapped
with tiny cracks,
intricate cloisonné.
I see latches, levers, pulls, handles.

There is particular beauty
and purpose in each.
But the array is too endless
for any one dream

till I think to
look beyond.
There,
of course,
a door.

I hear your voice
wise and sure
in death.
You say
(and I swear
you're nearly laughing),

it doesn't matter
which we choose.

Each opens
the Door.

Calling the Dog

Following messages left in leaves   soil   air
he wanders too far.
When I call   he pauses
quickening
to hurl fullness and glory
ahead of the self
like whales breach   tigers lunge   hawks soar.
There's nothing but an arc
between hearing his name and springing
toward the one who named him.

I want this completeness.
I want to feel 100 trillion cells spark
from my body in answer
to what we call spirit.
I want to taste
the shimmering voltage course
from every rock   tree   star.
A moment before reaching me
he unsprings,
back to golden fur and brown eyes
arriving tongue first.

Overheard Calls

The ordinary is mysterious to me.
How plants breathe out
what we need to breathe in
and how their leaves eat sunlight.
How radio waves careen
through buildings and bodies
making invisible fields speak.
How songs play
over and over in our heads,
a gift of memory
from ancestors who heard music
only as it was performed.
How we argue over eternity
because what's living
grows old and dies,
while styrofoam cups
and car tires persist beyond us.

It's mysterious
we can call one another
trusting our voices carry
exactly to the ear we seek,
as we'd like prayer to do.
If, before the phone's invention,
we'd sought out
a stranger or two from history,
a man laboring in the fields,
a woman weaving cloth,
telling them there would come a time
when anyone, anywhere
could speak to anyone, anywhere
and they'd hear close up

sorrow and delight in far off voices
that farmer, that weaver would rejoice
in the blessed device, seeing it
spread wisdom and compassion.
What a time to live in, they'd imagine.

I hear us come into this fullness.
On crowded streets I walk by
as people speak to distant ears
of seven billion selves.
Voices connect
across trembling waves.
It sounds mysterious
as quantum entanglement,
ordinary as love.

Acknowledgments

The following poems appeared in these publications, some with slight alterations.

Atlanta Review International Publication Prize *Haying: June 12* fall 2009

Bewildering Stories *Sacrifice* issue 446 2010

ChicagoPoetry.com *Breathing the Deepwater Horizon* day 96

Christian Science Monitor *Why the Window Washer Reads Poetry* February 21, 2010

Dirty Napkin *Hard Frost* issue 5 Dec 2008

Dressing Room Poetry Journal *Forgetting Names* issue 7, 2013

EarthSpeak Magazine *Why We Walk the Dogs* autumn 2009

Everything Stops and Listens Ohio Poetry Association anthology 2012 *Haying June 12, Why the Window Washer Reads Poetry*

Iodine Poetry Journal *Nest Unmade* fall/winter 2013-2014

J Journal *Locust* *spring* 2011

Lucidity *Chains, Bars* winter 2011

Mannequin Envy *Ruminating, Haying: June 10* fall 2008

Our Common Sufferings: An Anthology of World Poets in Memoriam 2008 Sichuan Earthquake *Doorways*

Poised in Flight anthology 2013 (Kind of a Hurricane Press) *So Soon*

Pudding Magazine *Tearing Down the Schoolhouse* winter 2013

Red River Review *Driving Through Fog* May 2013

Rose & Thorn Journal *A Pilgrimage* winter 2011
Shot Glass Journal *Dreams of Mice, New to the City*
    2013 issue 10
The Poet's Quest for God anthology 2013 *Overheard Calls*
The Shine Journal 2010 poetry contest, honorable mention
    Imaginary Boyfriends
Voices on the Wind *Perspective of Distance, Aluminum*
    Epiphany   issue 51

About the Author

Laura Grace Weldon has created collaborative poems with nursing home residents and taught nonviolence using poetry. She lives on Bit of Earth Farm in Ohio where she's a writer, editor, and marginally useful farm wench. She's the author of *Free Range Learning* and working on her next book, *Subversive Cooking.* Keep up with her at lauragraceweldon.com/blog-2/

Made in the USA
San Bernardino, CA
17 November 2013